URBAN ENTREPRENEUR

COMEDY

D1521028

Urban Entrepreneur: Comedy

Scobre Educational
2255 Calle Clara
La Jolla, CA 92037

Scobre Operations & Administration
42982 Osgood Road
Fremont, CA 94539

www.scobre.com
info@scobre.com

Scobre Educational publications may be purchased for
educational, business, or sales promotional use.

Cover and layout design by Jana Ramsay
Copyedited by Renae Reed
Some photos by Getty Images

ISBN: 978-1-61570-949-6 (E-Book)
ISBN: 978-1-61570-885-7 (Hard Cover)
ISBN: 978-1-61570-871-0 (Soft Cover)

TABLE OF CONTENTS

Chapter 1

What's So Funny?

Imagine you're telling a funny story to a group of friends. You watch as they all start laughing hysterically. You see them cracking up, grinning, wiping tears of laughter from their eyes—completely losing it.

Why are they reacting this way? They're all reacting to a shared experience of some kind, and the way you've turned it on its

An old saying goes, "Laughter is the best medicine." Scientific data suggests that the act of laughing can increase blood flow and improve the immune system.

head, or presented it in a new way. That, plus the way you said it, your expression, the words you chose to use—you nailed the delivery, and it's just *funny*!

But what *is* "funny?" To get a laugh out of anyone, you have to know what sort of things they think are funny. Successful comedians can connect to a group of people by presenting the world in ways you might not have thought of. The best comedians take these relatable

Many friends have inside jokes that only they understand.

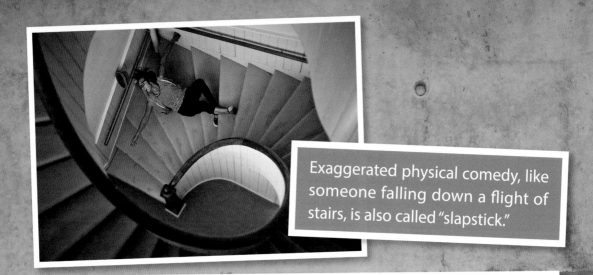

Exaggerated physical comedy, like someone falling down a flight of stairs, is also called "slapstick."

elements, twist them into knots for your entertainment, and mix in the element of irony. Irony is the expression of meaning by using language that normally signifies the opposite. For example, finding the humor in unfortunate events is a form of irony. If your friend falls down a flight of stairs, grunting and making funny noises every time he hits a step, this could be *ironically* funny. As long as he isn't seriously hurt, you both will probably start laughing the moment he stands back up.

Comedy has existed since the first person laughed, which was—well, a really long time ago. But as a form of entertainment, comedy began in the early 1900s, with vaudeville. Vaudeville was a type of "variety" entertainment, similar to many of today's late-night talk shows. It was made up of different acts; comedians were only one act in addition to musicians, dancers, magicians, acrobats, and even actors performing short skits or scenes from plays. The comedians in vaudevillian acts typically used simple subject matter and quirky characters to get the audience to laugh.

One of the most important figures in

comedic history came from vaudeville. His name was Julius "Groucho" Marx. Born in 1890, he began his vaudeville career as a singer in 1905, when a totally random event changed his life forever. In 1909, Julius Marx was part of a singing act with two of his brothers. Unfortunately, the trio wasn't very popular... Until one night, after a seriously *bad* performance, they started cracking jokes on stage—and the crowd loved it! Thanks to this one lucky performance, Marx and his brothers saw their opportunity for success—so they dropped the singing and became strictly a comedy act. The Marx brothers became one of the most famous vaudeville acts of all time, and they even went on to have three hit plays on Broadway. Broadway had *never* hosted an act that was solely comedy, so this was a huge deal—and a sign of things to come.

The Marx brothers' comedy acts were *beyond* popular… But why? What made them so funny? What people loved about the Marx brothers was their physical comedy, quick wordplay, and character acting. Julius ("Groucho"), and his brothers Leonard ("Chico") and Arthur ("Harpo") were Italian and Irish, and they played on all the stereotypes they knew audiences would relate to. Groucho was known for his quick-talking wise-guy character, who had a painted-on mustache and eyebrows, and large glasses. This is where the iconic costume "disguise" of fake eyeglasses with attached eyebrows, nose, and mustache comes from! Groucho used this "disguise" constantly. He understood that it was hilarious—because, of course, a person isn't really concealed by wearing the get-up. They just *think* they are.

Although comedians like the Marx brothers were known for being loud and fast-talking, comedy as a movement began slowly. Vaudeville gave comedy its first real venue, and it did well there; but the comedian still hadn't made it to

A scene from a 1890s vaudeville act in San Francisco.

center stage. However, it quickly became obvious that comedy would become way too popular for one venue. Soon, it was being performed in all sorts of places. And as the venues grew in the 1930s, '40s, and '50s, the variety of topics—and the star power of the comedians—grew, too. Entrepreneurs of comedy saw their chance to shine, and they jumped at it.

Since then, comedy has changed the world way more than most people think. When it comes to uncomfortable but important issues, comedians get the ball rolling by being unafraid to tackle those topics, and taking a stand for their opinions while they do. Comedy has

"I Love Lucy" was a very popular comedy show in the 1950s. Many critics consider Lucille Ball to be one of the greatest comedians of all time.

given performers a way to break down these barriers more than any other form of entertainment. From small folk clubs and theaters, to TV and radio, comedians keep putting new, bold material into their routines, and bringing them right into your home. Comedy became a vehicle for change, a place to have taboo discussions, and an open forum to discuss serious topics.

While comedy started out as a career mainly dominated by white performers, like Groucho Marx, that all changed during the 1970s. After the Civil Rights Movement, American culture was dominated by African Americans. Through their comedy acts, these talented performers were vital to Americans' views about race and equality. It was during this time that comedy changed into an actual career, and a form of entertainment all its own. To this day, stand-up comedy in the 1970s is mostly where our idea of "modern comedy" comes from.

Today, comedy is a truly cross-cultural medium, owned by anyone with the drive and talent for the comedic stage.

Comedian Tracy Morgan, from "Saturday Night Live" and "30 Rock," entertains a California crowd in 2014.

Chapter 2
Urban Comedy from Pryor to Murphy

In the 1970s, comedy made its way into American households. It was finally going mainstream, getting more conversational, talking about issues—and this all started with one person: Richard Pryor.

A lot of people call Pryor the "father" of modern comedy, and give him the credit for how popular it is today. Pryor started his rise to fame in the '60s and '70s, making a name for himself on the stand-up stage. From there, he went on to write and act for

comedy TV shows, like "Saturday Night Live." He even had a successful career as an actor. He starred in comedy films, and also acted alongside classic stars of the day, like Gene Wilder.

But all of Pryor's success didn't come easily. Like many kids at the time, Pryor didn't have the greatest childhood. But when he was 23, he decided he wanted to start fresh and pursue his dreams— so he moved to New York. There, he started performing in comedy clubs. He was talented, and people loved him, which let him book gigs alongside famous entertainers like Bob Dylan and Woody Allen.

But just like many of us, Pryor initially suffered from stage fright. His nerves were the *worst* right before going on stage. But he never let that stop him, and he overcame his nerves through sheer determination. Pryor knew he was good at making people laugh,

Pryor is eaten by the "Land Shark" in a popular "Saturday Night Live" skit from 1975.

and he loved it. So he did his best to beat his stage fright, and he didn't let it affect him. While he was new to the comedy scene, he made a name for himself by sticking to material that wasn't controversial, and focusing on his style and delivery. People loved the way his comedy told stories, and the way he made observations about the city and its people.

In 1967, though, after years of non-controversial topics and style, Pryor did something totally unexpected while performing live in Las Vegas. When he walked out on stage and saw a sold-out crowd, he began his act with a really controversial opening—and the crowd went wild! After this unexpected success paid off, he started to incorporate more controversial language and subjects into his comedy acts, taking on issues that other comedians wouldn't even touch. This became the legendary trademark of Pryor's brand of comedy—and the style that would shape comedy for years to come.

Pryor's talent was obvious to anyone who saw him perform, and in the 1960s, he got so popular that he started performing on hit TV shows, like "The Ed Sullivan Show" and "The Tonight Show". Later, he even began writing for TV, for "The Flip Wilson Show" and "Saturday Night Live." In fact, Pryor was the first-ever African-American host of SNL in 1975.

By the time 1977 rolled around, his success on TV led to the start of his very own show: "The Richard Pryor Show". However, its subject matter was too controversial for television, and it only aired a few episodes before it was canceled. But in the end, Pryor stood up for his content—he didn't change his vision for the show, or his comedic style, based on what the network's censors would approve.

This is one of the most basic facts of comedy: Comedians don't want to be censored. They are known for their controversial content, and that's one reason why they're always

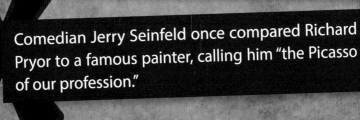

Comedian Jerry Seinfeld once compared Richard Pryor to a famous painter, calling him "the Picasso of our profession."

so popular. They push the envelope, toe the line. People love watching them take risks—risks that pay off with laughter, risks that are seriously entertaining. Unlike other performers, comedians can speak out about controversial issues in a much less formal setting, where the audience is ready to listen to—and most importantly, laugh about—sensitive subjects. By being open to the humor in these conversations, people can talk about issues like racism or class inequality in a way that is so much easier than a more serious setting would allow.

Sarah Silverman is another famous comedian who is known for pushing the envelope. She is famous for her edgy comedy that brings attention to many social issues.

Chapter 3
From Murphy, to TV, and beyond

And while Richard Pryor was one of the first to bring such controversial topics to the comedic stage, his sucessor Eddie Murphy followed right in Pryor's footsteps. Once again, Murphy made it clear that comedy was a place for controversial content.

Like Pryor, Murphy's childhood wasn't the greatest, either. His father passed away when he was young, and his mother later became too sick to take care of him and his brother. When Murphy was only eight years old, he and his brother were sent into foster care for a year, later returning home when his mother had gotten better. These tough times, so early in Murphy's life, greatly influenced his sense of humor. They gave him experiences that helped developed his comedic style. He learned to look back on those hard times, and find ways to laugh about them. And when you can look back at a bad situation and find something funny about it, that's a form of comedy that people can really relate to.

When he was only 15 years old, Murphy started writing and performing comedy routines. He was influenced by other great African-American comedians, like Richard

Pryor (of course!), and Bill Cosby. Murphy, like Pryor, became known for his use of strong language and controversial topics, including making fun of different groups of people for laughs. Pryor said that he found Murphy's comedy "insensitive" sometimes. But despite this, Murphy made a name for himself in comedy clubs in California's Bay Area. Even while he was still fairly new to performing, he did performances at the same club frequented by Robin Williams and Whoopi Goldberg.

In addition to being an actor, Eddie Murphy is also a singer. He was able to show off both talents in the 2006 musical "Dreamgirls."

Murphy made such a huge name for himself in the comedy clubs, he eventually snagged a spot as a regular actor on "Saturday Night Live." His performances on SNL helped to revitalize the show during the early '80s. One of his most famous characters included a spoof of the beloved children's show host from the 1980s, Mr. Rogers. Instead, "Mr. Robinson" was a poor but street-wise version. And Murphy also played a jaded and cynical version of Gumby, the animated character.

In 1982, Eddie Murphy became the first regular Saturday Night Live cast member to host the show. The originally scheduled host, Nick Nolte, was too sick to perform, so Murphy filled in for him.

Richard Pryor and Eddie Murphy both used stand-up comedy to launch themselves into the TV industry. They made a name for themselves in movies, too—where, previously, African Americans had been unfairly overlooked on the big screen. But even as these two talented comedians broke into the movie industry, both Murphy and Pryor were often cast alongside white co-stars. Murphy was cast alongside

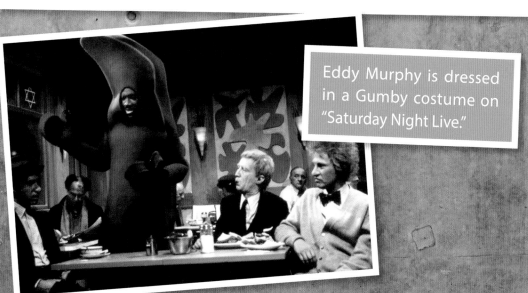

Eddy Murphy is dressed in a Gumby costume on "Saturday Night Live."

Nick Nolte in "48 Hrs.," and Pryor was cast alongside Gene Wilder in "Stir Crazy" and "Blazing Saddles", among other films.

Murphy aimed to change all that.

Murphy's popularity skyrocketed during his comedy career—especially thanks to "Saturday Night Live." Viewers got excited about seeing Murphy on TV. It's not a huge surprise that the prominence of African Americans in comedy had a very positive impact on the country's

Eddie Murphy accepts a Screen Actors Guild Award in 2007.

developing views of equality. As a result, Americans finally began to appreciate the diversity and talent African Americans had to offer—in comedy, on TV, and in movies. *Finally*, the entertainment industry was ready to set aside its prejudice and accept African Americans into leading roles in the business.

Thanks to his success in his comedy career, with his stand-up and on SNL, he then moved on to the film industry, playing humorous street-smart characters. Murphy's first big-screen role was co-starring in a film called "48 Hrs." The movie was a big success. He continued in the film industry with "Trading Places" in

1983, and then "Beverly Hills Cop" in 1984. "Beverly Hills Cop" was Murphy's first truly starring role. His character was originally set to be played by Sylvester Stallone. But thanks to Murphy, the film was one of the most successful movies in history. "Beverly Hills Cop" still ranks in the top 50 highest-grossing films in the U.S., which is a *huge* deal, considering how many movies have been made since it was released in 1984!

Other signs of America's changing views were everywhere. "In Living Color" was a comedy show that came to TV in 1990. It was another sketch

The name, "In Living Color," was inspired by the early color television broadcasts of the 1950s and 1960s. The name also refers to the diversity of the show's cast.

Keenen, Marlon, and Damon Wayans pose at the first-ever BET Comedy Awards in 2004.

comedy show, like SNL. But its cast was made up of mainly African American comedians. Its creators, Keenen and Damon Wayans, recognized the impact African-Americans were having in the comedy business. Though they weren't comedians themselves, the Wayans brothers saw an opportunity to meet America's demand for this type of entertainment. They created "In Living

Color"—and their entrepreneurial spirit paid off. "In Living Color" was a huge success, and it acted as the gateway for many comedians to show off their talents. Actors like Jamie Foxx and Jim Carrey were guests on the show, and went on to have huge careers in film and comedy. In 1991, future superstar Jennifer Lopez was cast as a dancer on the show—her very first high-profile job.

Jennifer Lopez was honored with a Hollywood Walk of Fame star in 2013.

Chapter 4
Comedy Goes Mainstream

Murphy, Pryor, and all the other entrepreneurs in the comedy business had huge obstacles in front of them as they tried to establish their careers. But once they had blazed that trail, comedy was solidified as a nationwide, popular, *stand-alone* form of entertainment. Many comedians started their careers with the goal of being on TV or in movies. But what about someone who just wants to be a comedian? Finally, this was possible.

As a successful comedian *and* actor, Murphy helped to make this dream possible. One night, Murphy saw someone performing stand-up in a nightclub—this person was obviously talented, so Murphy became his friend and mentor. Who was this new comedian? Chris Rock.

Thanks to Murphy, Rock landed his first film role, in "Beverly Hills Cop II," in 1987. Rock ended up using his success in film (and TV) to build his *comedy* career, instead of the other way around.

In 1990, after his role in "Beverly Hills Cop II", Rock joined the cast of "Saturday Night

Live." His performances there were a huge success. Rock and a few other SNL cast members, including Adam Sandler, were so popular and talented, they were called the "Bad Boys of SNL."

From there, he made his way back to where he started—where he *really* wanted to be—stand-up comedy. In 1993, Rock left SNL and appeared briefly on "In Living Color." But unfortunately, the show was almost over, and it ended a few months after Rock arrived. After that, he decided to try his hand at film again, but this didn't work out either. So he went back to his home in stand-up—and he came back *strong*!

In 1996, Rock's stand-up special "Bring the Pain" was a huge success. He won two

Emmy Awards for his performance, and was recognized as one of America's greatest comedians. His most-discussed act was one that focused on race in America, and Rock used strong language to make his points—just like Pryor and Murphy before him.

Rock's success continued in 1999 and 2004 with two new HBO comedy specials. These specials presented a unique opportunity for Rock—why not take his new comedy specials on tour, like bands do with their new albums? This enterprising business venture paid off, and Rock's comedy tours were a huge success—he sold out entire stadiums, something that would have been unheard of just 50 years ago.

But how is Rock so popular? How does he know what will be funny? Well, Rock does something unique with his new material—he tests it out in smaller comedy clubs before taking it to his larger audiences. That way, he knows which jokes people will like better, and what he still needs to work on.

Thanks to Rock's huge success, *Time* magazine and *Entertainment Weekly* named him "the funniest man in America." Rock also wrote and hosted his own television show,

"The Chris Rock Show," which featured interviews with celebrities and political figures. His television success won him three Emmy Awards, and 15 nominations, and all because he was focusing on what he knew best—stand-up comedy. Today, thanks to all of this popularity and acclaim, Rock is considered one of the greatest stand-up comedians of this generation.

Chris Rock hosted the 77th Annual Academy Awards in 2005.

Today, thanks to the work of entrepreneurial comedians before him, Rock is able to be a *comedian*. His comedy shows fill up 50,000-seat stadiums—a huge step up from those little vaudeville acts of the past!

But what's next? What does someone have to do now, today, to get into comedy? The answer is one that might surprise you.

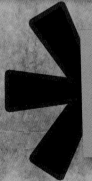

Many former stars from "Saturday Night Live" have gone on to have successful TV comedy shows of their own. Tina Fey starred in "30 Rock," and Amy Poehler leads a hilarious cast in "Parks and Recreation."

There are almost limitless ways to share media online.

With social media and websites that allow you to share your content with the click of a button, it's easier than ever to find an audience for your comedic genius.

Whoever you are, wherever you're from, whatever your specific "brand" of comedy—today is the time get out there and own it. Who knows? Maybe the next YouTube sensation is a comedian like you.

Are you ready?